WHAT'S NEXT FOR ENTERTAINMENT?

Tom Jackson

WAYLAND

First published in 2013 by Wayland

Copyright © Wayland 2013

Wayland
Hachette Children's Books
338 Euston Road
London NW1 3BH

Wayland Australia
Level 17/207 Kent Street
Sydney NSW 2000

Senior editor: Julia Adams
Editor: Annabel Stones
Designer: Maddox Philpot
Illustrator: Maddox Philpot
Consultant: Sean Connolly
        Proofreader & Indexer: Kay Barnham

Picture acknowledgements:
p. 7 (top): ZUMA Press, Inc./Alamy;
p. 11 (top): ZUMA Press, Inc./Alamy;
p. 17 (bottom): c.Focus Features/
Everett/Rex Features; p. 24 (bottom):
Matthew Salacuse/Corbis Outline.

Dewey classification: 790

ISBN: 978 0 7502 7799 0

Printed in China

Wayland is a division of Hachette
Children's Books,
an Hachette UK Company.

www.hachette.co.uk

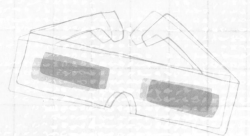

ENTERTAINMENT SCIENCE NOW

Games and sports are as old as human civilisation. Long ago they were good practice for staying alive. Games require players to plan ahead and imagine which possible moves their opponents might make. Sports are based on fighting or hunting skills, which were once essential. Do we still play in the same way today?

Leisure time

We seldom think it, but most of us have more free time than ever before. Just over a century ago, adults – and their older children too – worked for 60 hours a week, often with only one day off every now and then. Today, the average working week is half as long.

HANGING OUT WITH FRIENDS

All that free time means that we need a lot of entertainment. Humans are very talkative, and so we spend a lot of our free time chatting to each other — often about other people. Communication technology means that we can gossip with friends all over the world at the same time.

Seeing is believing

A lot of our entertainment today requires a screen. High-definition screens mean that our films and television programmes are clearer and sharper than ever — almost as if we were there. However, technology will find new ways to make the viewing experience even more real. Meanwhile computer graphics and clever programs put game players into the heart of the action. In future, we will be able to have even more control over what goes on in the game, perhaps creating our own characters that 'live' inside it.

Into the future

People are always looking for new ways to have fun and we can only guess at what the future holds. In this book, we'll use the latest research to take a look into the future and suggest how today's scientific ideas might change the way we live in the years to come. An icon next to each technology that we introduce will give you an idea of when they may become a part of our daily lives.

PLAYING AROUND

Tag is an example of a game that doesn't really need any technology. But then someone invented laser tag, where you zap your opponents instead of touching them. In future, new technology could transform other old games and perhaps create some new ones.

Robot pets

5 YEARS

People keep pets because they want to have an animal to play with, to look after and which loves them back. There are already robot pets that need care and attention straight out of the box. In future, robot pets will become cheaper, tougher and more agile, but they will also become cleverer, programmed to be curious and find things to play with by themselves.

Hide and seek

15 YEARS

Technology could make a game of hide and seek a lot more fun. Armies around the world are developing cloaks that make you invisible. The material is a flexible screen, with cameras dotted all over it. These record the view behind you and then show it on the front of the cloak (the back shows the view from the front). So someone looking for you will see right through you! Hiding will be easier than ever. However, finding will be easier too, thanks to radar goggles. These emit radio beams that are tuned to bounce off living bodies. The beams travel through walls (and cloaks) to detect people behind them, who then appear in the goggle display.

Game drones

Drones are aircraft that can fly on their own, following a preset program or instructions from a controller on the ground. Drones are already used by governments and companies, but soon they could be used for fun. The sky is the limit for drone games. We could race them, use them on treasure hunts or just go on adventures - all via a video link. Solar-powered drones can fly for days (or years!) without ever having to land (at night they run on battery power). Your game drone could take you all over the world.

`10 YEARS`

Toy drones will be powered by propellers, and could be the size of a dragonfly!

GET A LITTLE LOST

`5 YEARS`

Technology could even change a simple stroll. Apps called 'chance engines' will add in a bit of excitement as you take a walk along the same old streets. They will suggest new routes, taking you to places in your neighbourhood that you've never been to before. These apps could also set challenges to add fun to your walk — perhaps telling you to touch every postbox you see, or spot to five people who are wearing hats. Adding a bit more chance into our lives may mean we will make new friends and have more fun.

! ERROR ALERT

Spoiling games

One of the first things computer scientists did was to teach their computers how to play games. Computers are good at following rules and so they are good at games — in fact, they are too good. If you play draughts, noughts and crosses or Connect 4 against a computer, you will never win. The computer already knows every possible move in the game. Supercomputers can already beat the best chess players as well. However, teaching computers to be so good at games has shown scientists how to develop more intelligent machines, which could help us in many more serious ways than games...

COMPUTER GAMING

Computers revolutionised games, taking players into new worlds on screen that were filled with characters they could control. Future gaming revolutions might do the opposite – turn the real world into a game!

A new layer

NOW!

Our smartphones and tablets will turn the world around us into a game zone. The system uses AR - 'augmented reality' - which puts an extra layer of images on top of what you can see through the gadget's camera. AR games could make the local park into a treasure island or turn city landmarks into alien invaders that players in the area must team up to defeat.

ALL IN THE MIND

25 YEARS

Games are all about brain over brawn - it is the cleverest player who wins, not the strongest. In future, games will pick up our brainwaves - the electrical activity inside our heads - using the same kind of detectors that doctors use today. This will allow us to have brain battles, where, for example, players compete to have the calmest mind. A blink creates a spike in brainwaves, so could be a 'fire' command, perhaps sending balls towards the opponent's goal on screen. The opponent must not get too worried about this. Remaining calm means that he can fire the balls back again - even faster. Eventually, the excitement will get the better of someone.

Video floor

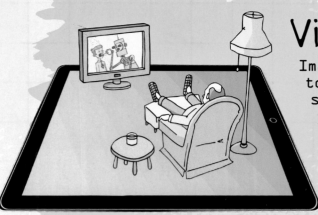

15 YEARS

Imagine a floor that is also a touch-sensitive screen. Looking down, you see a mirror image of the real room around you. The floor knows who you are from your weight and so a virtual version of you is down there as well. Floor screens are likely to be common in the homes of the future. Just imagine, they would let you kick a virtual ball around the house — and never break anything!

Nail screen

5 YEARS

Playing a game on a small touch screen can be difficult — your fingers get in the way and you can't see what is going on. How about wearing nail-sized screens on your fingertips? The screens display what is being hidden by your fingers — so you can see right through them.

⚠ ERROR ALERT

Better than computers

Strange as it may sound, some mathematical problems are impossible to solve on a computer. They were created to follow instructions, but the instructions on how to solve some problems mean the computer has to do an almost infinite number of calculations that would literally take for ever to complete. Humans are better at this kind of thing because we know which parts of the problem to concentrate on — and can ignore the rest. However, a computer may still come in handy. A 'hard' problem, such as figuring out the different ways protein molecules might fit together, is programmed as a puzzle computer game. Human players are more efficient at finding possible solutions, while a computer solving the same problem would try every possible combination in turn.

TOYS OF THE FUTURE

Toys are not just for fun; they are a way for children to learn how to control their bodies so that they can use grown-up tools and equipment one day. As technology changes how adults live, children's toys will change too.

Shape-shifters

`20 YEARS`

Transforming robot toys have been around for decades — they even star in their own films. But American scientists have developed a robot that can transform all by itself. Its body is made up of magnetic units that can be turned on to stick together and off again to break apart. Some of the units contain stronger magnets than others, and so can push and pull the weaker ones around, folding and twisting them into new shapes. One day we may find this technology in toys — you could set up an obstacle course for your robot and it would transform into the best shape to move through each section.

Soft-toy software

Even cuddly toys will be high-tech in the future. `5 YEARS` They will have screens and internet connections so that young children could communicate with each other. There would need to be high safety precautions though. One could be that two toddlers would only be able to connect online once their cuddly toys had exchanged a short-distance radio signal by being right next to each other.

PAUSE FOR THOUGHT

Is it good for small children to have friends online or should we keep them away from screen technology until they are a bit older?

10

Print your toys

Many children and adults enjoy making models and there are lots of kits available. In 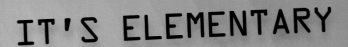 future you won't need to go and buy the components. You can just print them with your 3D printer. All you'll need to do is download the design and send it to print. You could even design your own kits.

5 YEARS

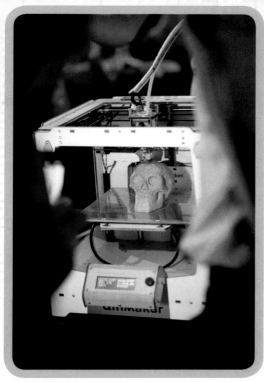

A 3D printer in action.

IT'S ELEMENTARY

3D printing

3D printing makes use of inkjet technology that has been around for many years. But, instead of squirting out tiny dots of ink, like an everyday inkjet printer does, 3D printers are filled with liquid plastic. When this plastic meets the air, it goes solid, and that means new layers of plastic can be printed on top, gradually building up just about any 3D shape.

BATH BOTS

10 YEARS

Robots do not all have clanking metal arms and legs. Soft, flexible robots are being developed that are filled with liquid. They move around, like a worm or a jellyfish, by squeezing one part of the body so the liquid inside flows to another part, so that it gets longer or changes shape. One day we might play with a robot jellyfish in the bath instead of a plastic duck.

TELLING STORIES

Stories are much older than paper and books – we used to tell them to each other and not write them down at all. As new technology replaces printed words and pictures, stories will still be there, but we may tell them in different ways.

Wandering tales

As paper pages give way to screens, the structure of stories will change. Hypertext links, like the ones we use to click around the internet, will make it possible to choose which bits of a story to read first. The links could allow you to explore every aspect of the different characters or take you straight to all the exciting bits of the plot. You could re-read books and find out new things every time.

Bendy screens

The difference between paper and a screen will not be so clear in future. A flexible plastic screen can be rolled or folded like a piece of paper, but does not always show the same words and pictures. You could even write on it. Today's screen pictures are formed by dots of light from LEDs – light-emitting diodes. A flexible screen will do the same, but will use OLEDs – organic light-emitting diodes – instead, which do not snap when you bend them.

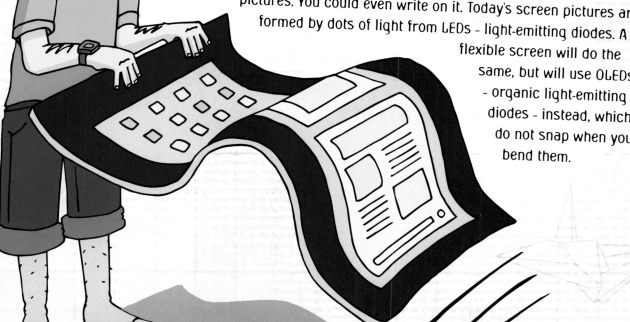

Video comics

10 YEARS

The images in comics and graphic novels make the story really come alive. In future, comic books could have video and sound as well as words. The paper has ultra-thin electronic components printed onto it. They could be screens that show an important action, such as a short cartoon video, or speakers that produce background sounds as you read. The pictures could even be printed with perfumed inks to give off the smells of a certain scene.

IT'S ELEMENTARY

Touchscreen technology

Small touchscreens, like those on a tablet or games console, have a see-through layer on the front of the screen that is electrically charged. A touch from a fingertip changes the amount of charge stored in that region of the screen, so the software knows where you are pressing. Touchscreens are generally controlled with 'soft keys'. These are like the keys on a keyboard, but they are only flashed up as images when you need them.

Write your own stories

10 YEARS

Computer games follow a story - one where players are the characters. In future, human players will create characters controlled by artificial intelligence that are left to interact with each other - and make up a story as they go along. The fun will be to watch your creation as it travels through the game world populated with characters created by other players. The result will be an epic tale where no one knows what will happen - the end has not been written yet.

WATCHING SCREENS

The TV was invented almost 100 years ago, and it is hard to imagine life without screens in our homes. But will we also need a screen for catching up with our favourite programmes? Let's take a look at how watching TV might change in future.

3D anywhere

We've all seen 3D movies at the cinema, sitting in the dark and wearing special glasses. The same kind of system is used in today's 3D televisions. There are glasses-free versions, but you have to sit right in front of the screen — hard luck if you are at the wrong end of the couch. A new system is being developed that can direct a 3D image at any person in the room. The special TV screen divides the picture up into hundreds of slices that are sent out in all directions in front of the screen. Wherever you are sitting each eye will pick up one image slice — and the brain turns them into a 3D image, just as it does with a view of the real world.

10 YEARS

IT'S ELEMENTARY

Stereoscopy

3D video is based on a system called stereoscopy. The right eye sees a slightly different view of the world to the left. Each one can only see in 2D, but the brain uses the slight differences in the two images to create a 3D view. A 3D screen sends out two slightly different images – one for the left and one for the right eye. The glasses we wear ensure that the correct image reaches the correct eye; the other is blocked. And – as if by magic – the flat objects rise up out of the screen into a 3D image.

LIVE IN YOUR LIVING ROOM

WATCHING TOGETHER

About 30 years ago, when the television set was the only screen in most houses, the whole family watched television together. Today we can watch programmes more or less anywhere and anytime, and we often do it on our own. Social networking apps will soon coordinate groups of friends so they can all watch their favourite TV programme together. When you turn on a particular show, the app alerts your friends so they can watch it with you wherever they are in the world and chat about what they see – just like in olden times!

2 YEARS

HOLOCUBE

20 YEARS

The idea of having a holographic television is not a new one, but it is proving a difficult technology to develop. A hologram is a 3D image that you can walk around — so you can see a front and a back. A holographic TV — or holovision set — would be in the middle of the living room and you could watch the action from any direction. One hologram system being developed uses a block of plastic sheets, each of which can display a slice of the overall 3D image. Crucially, this system can change the image slices very quickly — many times a second — which means that the hologram can move in a lifelike way.

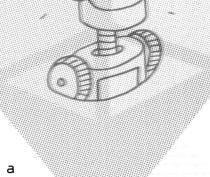

SENSOVISION

One day we will do more than watch television - we'll feel it, too. Skin tight bodysuits could stimulate the different sensors in the skin, creating sensations of pain, touch, hot or cold. Just as a soundtrack is cued up to match the moving pictures on screen, a sensotrack would mean you felt the same things as a character on screen - you could even choose which one you wanted to be.

20 YEARS

ON THE BIG SCREEN

Time to go to the movies – so called because they show moving pictures. (The word 'cinema' comes from the Greek word for 'movement'). Movies have been around since the 1890s, and in the 1920s we got the 'talkies' when you could hear what the actors were saying as well. In future, might we go to the 'smellies' or the 'feelies'?

Surround screen

10 YEARS

Cinema screens are getting bigger all the time. The world's largest is in Sydney, Australia, and is the size of four tennis courts. Instead of getting bigger and bigger, screens of the future may be curved into domes that surround the audience. A few experimental cinema domes have been built already. A central projector means that the action comes from all directions, so the audience will be free to walk around inside and experience movies in a whole new way.

STACKS OF FACTS

An IMAX movie projector uses a 50-cm light bulb made of super-strong fused quartz and pumped full of high-pressure xenon gas. If the light bulb cracked, it would explode, so projectionists must wear protective body armour when they change it.

The first nature documentary was shown in cinemas in 1903. It showcased the lives of microscopic mites that lived on a lump of cheese.

Early movie film was made from transparent nitrocellulose with the images or frames printed on top. Nitrocellulose is also used as an explosive called guncotton, and as films aged they decayed into highly flammable dust, which could explode without warning - and often did.

The first movie to be shown in Smell-O-Vision was *Scent of Mystery* in 1960, starring Elizabeth Taylor. Cues on the film triggered odours to be pumped throughout the auditorium to match the scenes on screen. The system was a failure. No other Smell-O-Vision movie was made.

Interactive movies

One day, the cinema audience will become  part of the action. Motion sensors in the screen will monitor the location of people in the auditorium and represent them as characters on screen, giving them tasks to do or allowing them to control how the story develops.

SEAT SENSORS

Gadgets that were originally developed to add extra sensations during computer games could one day become part of normal cinema seats. They will take advantage of the body's senses to create fear or excitement. The cinema seat might exude scent chemicals to match the scenes on screen, but human noses are not very sensitive. Our skin is though, and small vibrating probes could create a range of spooky sensations. For example, hard, slow pulses on the skin feel like rain, and faster, softer pulses a small distance apart create an eerie stroking sensation, as if you are being touched by an invisible hand. Aaarrgh!

Printer characters

Stop-motion animations like *Wallace and Gromit* have a great look that is different from cartoony computer graphics. But they take a very long time to make. One second of film takes about a day to shoot, as animators make tiny adjustments to the characters' bodies and faces. In future, the process could be speeded up by printing 3D models of the characters' faces and swapping one for another in each scene. The 2009 film *Coraline* used this technique, with every smile and scowl of the main character planned on computer.

Coraline was perhaps the first movie star to have a printed face.

NOW!

17

LISTENING TO MUSIC

Music is just waves in the air that follow a special pattern. We record sound by converting those waves into electrical signals. To play back our recording we simply wobble the air in just the right way to recreate the tuneful sounds. Let's look at how future audio technology might do more than play our top tracks.

Anything is a loudspeaker

Recorded music needs a loudspeaker to turn it into sound. A loudspeaker is a movable surface that is made to vibrate by the electrical recording - and that creates the sound waves. In future, we could turn just about any surface into a speaker - a tabletop, a door, or even a bottle - we just need to add vibrations. Those would come by attaching a block of terbium metal, which can be made to expand and contract using magnets. Electrical signals control the magnets; which make the terbium vibrate - and you have sound.

`20 YEARS`

VOICE IN A CROWD

`5 YEARS`

At large festivals and outdoor concerts, it is hard to hear music clearly. Some sounds travel further than others – and noise from elsewhere can get in the way – so you only hear half the music if you are far away. In future, concert goers might all listen to music sent to their phones. The sound from the stage is transmitted by radio so that music lovers hear it in better quality. The system will delay the sound according to how far away the listener is, taking into account the speed of sound going out from the live version. People at the back of the arena will hear the sound a little later than those right at the front. Without this function, the live version would be out of step with the radio feed.

Healthy music

NOW!

In future, we may listen to music for more than just pleasure – it will keep us healthy too. Researchers in Japan found that mice that had had major operations were healthier if they listened to music. The trial showed that Mozart's music was healthier than listening to songs by Enya, but that was still much better than just listening to a tuneless hum.

Sharing the dance

3 YEARS

A DJ in a nightclub wants to play music that the dancers will like. But how does he or she know? In future, the guests' music players will transmit their top playlists to the club computer when they arrive. The computer can then figure out what to play to attract the most people onto the dance floor. Who needs a DJ?

! ERROR ALERT

Earworms

Have you ever caught an earworm? Don't worry, it is not a real worm, just an expression for when you get a catchy tune stuck in your head and you can't stop humming it to yourself. The brain is very good at remembering different melodies — you do it without thinking, so one day earworms might be put to use as reminders of important information. One suggestion is to play catchy melodies on different levels of large car parks. If you forget where you left your car, just listen out for a familiar tune.

PERFORMING MUSIC

Music is perhaps the oldest of all art forms. No one knows for sure, but it is likely that as early humans developed speech, they also learned to sing. We've been performing music ever since. Let's look at how future technology will help us do it.

Evolving melodies

NOW!

A person who writes music is called a composer – they have an amazing ability to find new melodies. In future, we might write music in a different way – by evolving it. 'Darwin music' is an internet experiment where listeners are played short loops of music and they rate each one. The unpopular loops are thrown out and popular ones are tweaked by computer, adding a few new sounds. Then the process happens again. Over many generations of loops, the music 'evolves' into a great tune.

PAUSE FOR THOUGHT

Evolving music creates melodies by asking for everyone's opinion. Is this always the best way to produce something or can one person working on his or her own do it better?

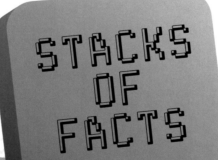

STACKS OF FACTS

In 1994, British rocker Rod Stewart played a concert to 4.2 million people on Copacabana Beach in Rio de Janeiro, Brazil - the largest music performance in history.

The Was 3000 loudspeaker can produce 165 decibels which is louder than a jet engine, and enough to shake people so much they are sick!

The coronation of Tsar Alexander II in 1856 included an underwater concert, where musicians played underwater inside a submarine in Kronstadt harbour. Their music filled the water and was easily audible on land.

Mould music

Slime mould is a type of fungus, a bit like yoghurt. Small electrical currents flow through the gooey life form, and researchers from Plymouth, England, are using this current to make musical tones. The mould also reacts to light – the electrical activity goes up and down as light flashes on and off – and that changes the tune. It is possible that future musical instruments will contain slime moulds that are played with flashing lights.

10 YEARS

Musical gestures

The latest games consoles use motion-capture technology so we can control the action just by moving our bodies. A futuristic musical instrument might make use of the same system to detect how it moves as it is played - and turn that into an extra layer of sound. For example, the angle of a violin bow as it strokes across a string might alter the sound of the note produced, or swaying a flute from side to side in time to the music might create a drumbeat.

2 YEARS

ROBOT CHOIR

Singing in groups is great fun, but most people are a bit shy about doing it solo. Robot singers are being developed that can sing along with us. First the robots listen to you sing and learn the melody. They then join in and sing in harmony with you. The robots also listen to each other and never sing the same part. Each robot chooses its part from a library of musical phrases programmed in by real-life musicians.

10 YEARS

NEW SPORTS

When does a game become a sport? There is no easy answer, but in general a sport requires strength, speed and physical skill – and some tactical thinking. Let's take a look at some ways we might compete against each other in future.

Team game

20 YEARS

Doctors are researching how the brain controls the body - especially muscle movements. This knowledge might be used to help disabled people get around better. However, it could also lead to a type of sport where one player controls the body of another by sending signals straight to their teammate's brain. The perfect team would be a strong athletic player whose body is used in the game, and a partner who is an expert in tactics and strategy. The teams might race along complex courses, solving puzzles and performing feats of strength as they go. Which player would you want to be?

PAUSE FOR THOUGHT

Is taking control of someone else's body always a good thing? When do you think it should be allowed?

ROBOT SOCCER

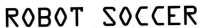

10 YEARS

Teams of robots have been playing football on small indoor courts for almost 20 years now — there is even a World Cup competition. The real players are the human programmers. As well as building fast robots that can move around without falling over, the human managers also need to teach their robots to find the ball and kick it — hopefully at the goal. Then they have to add in team tactics and extra skills. Today's robot teams are not very good — but perhaps in future our sporting heroes will be robots.

SPACEBALL

30 YEARS

One day, sports could be played in large satellites in orbit around Earth. In orbit, gravity does not make a ball fall down to the ground – it just keeps on going until it hits something! So a spaceball arena need not be flat. It could be a sphere, not with two goals but six. Six goals needs six teams, who would fly up from Earth for each match. But what would the rules be? Could teams gang up against each other? Could players fly around, propelled by little jets of air, or just push themselves away from the walls?
We'll have to wait and see.

Rally running

15 YEARS

Exoskeletons are robots that you can wear. They are being developed to help paralysed people walk and to help soldiers carry heavy kit and run faster on the battlefield. It is only a matter of time before exoskeletons are used in sport as well. Just as rally teams compete to build the best cars for racing on rugged courses today, one day we might see runners using exoskeletons to boost their speed and strength in extreme cross-country races.

IT'S ELEMENTARY

WEIGHTLESSNESS

We've all seen pictures of astronauts floating around their spacecraft. How do they manage it? Well, it is wrong to say there is no gravity in orbit – it is just weaker than down on the ground. Gravity is pulling the spacecraft down as well, but it is moving so fast around the world – more than 7 km a second! – that it never actually falls to Earth, it just keeps on going around and around. Anyone inside move at the same speed as the spacecraft. They are in orbit as well – and so just float around inside.

EXTREME SPORTS

Technology will not just make today's games faster or more exciting – it may be used to invent completely new leisure activities. Let's take a look at some extreme possibilities.

Spacediving

Felix Baumgartner is famous as a daredevil skydiver and BASE jumper. In 2012 he became known for something else – spacediving. He leapt from a balloon floating 39 km above the surface of Earth and zoomed down to the ground in the fastest freefall ever. One day spacediving could replace skydiving, and thrill-seekers could take a high-tech space elevator to the edge of space before plunging back to Earth.

100 YEARS

Air biking

Mountain bikers like to test themselves against the toughest terrain around - cycling over snowy peaks and into volcanic craters. What will be next? Perhaps the bikes will leave the ground completely. Every year inventors enter the Icarus Cup - a competition in England to see who can fly the furthest using an aircraft powered only by the human body. Better designs for cycle-copters and pedal-powered aircraft are tested out each year, built from super-strong but super-light materials. One day we might be going for ride not just in the country but over it as well.

20 YEARS

Felix Baumgartner set a new word record for the fastest freefall.

IT'S ELEMENTARY

THE SPACE ELEVATOR

Getting into space using a rocket requires a lot of expensive fuel. Going in a lift would be much cheaper. Although it would need a lot of energy to travel upwards – and each journey would take several hours – the downwards journey would not need power because of the pull of gravity, but would generate electricity used in the next upwards run. All we need now is for a super-strong, super-light material from which to make the elevator shaft – it would have to be many thousands of kilometres long.

Gecko climbing

5 YEARS

Geckos have super-sticky feet that allow them to walk up walls and across ceilings. Their feet don't exude glue, but are covered in ultra-fine feathery hairs, which grip the surface. Gloves and boots made out of a copycat hair-covered material have been developed. One day people will be able to climb just like a gecko. Watch out, though - you could still fall.

Water-jet pack

3 YEARS

Going swimming with a jet pack might not sound a good idea, but a new water-jet sport has been developed that means you do just that. A powerful pump worn on the back sucks up water through a long hose and then jets it out of the bottom of special boots. The result is that you rise up into the air. With a bit of practice, you can fly across the surface or just hover. If you slip up, the worst that can happen is that you fall into the water with a big splash!

WATCHING SPORTS

Perhaps the most common sporting activity is being a spectator. In other words watching other people do it. Whatever new sports there are in the future, technology will help us to enjoy watching them even more.

Robot film crew

When a big game is shown on television, a highly skilled director is in charge of keeping the action on screen by switching between several cameras, then replaying the highlights from the best angles. But this requires a lot of people and is too expensive to do for all games in one day. In future, robots do it all under the control of a central computer. Cameras will automatically follow the ball or stick to certain players, while the system cuts to different views as the players move around.

5 YEARS

Smart sports kit

Sports fans never grow tired of statistics: who hits the ball hardest; who runs the most in the game; who scores the most points. In future, sports stars may wear sensors on their kit that record their every move. As well as providing information to the spectators, the coaching staff could use the same system to monitor hard tackles, and to substitute players who get a bad knock.

5 YEARS

AI COMMENTATING

2 YEARS

Sports commentators are paid to talk. They work hard to tell us what is going on during the game and to give us some background about players in between the action. But sometimes they run out of things to say. That will all end thanks to an artificial-intelligence system that monitors the progress of the game and players. It will also find interesting anecdotes or statistics about when a similar thing happened in the past or what is most likely to happen next.

STACKS OF FACTS

The UK power grid requires an extra 3 gigawatts during half-time of a big England football match. As the players take a rest, millions of TV viewers switch the kettle on.

The Mexican wave is performed by spectators at sporting events. The longest ever recorded lasted nearly 7 minutes at an Australian basketball game in 2011.

The first sports commentator was Henry Blythe Thornhill Wakelam who described a rugby game between England and Wales on BBC radio in 1927. A colleague called out grid references from a diagram of the pitch printed in the Radio Times, so listeners knew where the ball was.

In the action

15 YEARS

Spectators are always looking for the best view of their favourite sport. A new headset will put the viewer right in the middle of the action. Cameras above the sports field provide a 360° view of the action. However, our eyes only have a 200° field of vision — we can't see behind us. Not unless we have the latest headset viewer, which squashes the entire scene into the human field view. Tests show that it takes a while to get used to seeing the world in this way, but it would give an unrivalled view of all the action — as if you were sitting right among the players.

TAKING A BREAK

The future is going to be so much fun, we won't ever want to take a break! Well, that may be true, but here are a few ideas of how the future of holidays might look.

Space hotel

`40 YEARS`

Forget the beach. In future, we might spend a few nights in a space hotel. Getting a big spacecraft into orbit requires a big rocket. That is why today's space stations are way too small to be hotels. However, one idea is to launch space balloons, which are folded up very small for launch and then puffed up with air to many times their size once in orbit. Inside, there will be plenty of room for paying guests. The balloon material is the same stuff used in bulletproof vests to ensure they don't burst.

Asteroid resort

`100 YEARS`

Mining companies are examining ways of landing crews on asteroids to find valuable minerals. The same systems could later be used to set up holiday resorts on asteroids that orbit near Earth. Time on an asteroid will be a lot of fun. Hikers could bound around in the low gravity, looking at the wonderful view and watching ice geysers that are set off by sunlight. Because asteroids are not round, their force of gravity pulls towards the largest mass – and that means balls can roll uphill! That would make a golfing holiday interesting.

IT'S ELEMENTARY

GRAVITY

This is the most obvious force of nature. It gives us our weight and ensures that what goes up does come down. Gravity is a force of attraction that pulls every object in the universe together. The nearer the objects are to each other, the stronger the pull. Just as importantly, larger masses pull harder than smaller ones. So you are not just being pulled down by the Earth – you are pulling the Earth up to you. But because the Earth is so much bigger, it doesn't really move at all.

Augmented-reality staycation

10 YEARS

They say a change is as good as a rest and in future we can go on holiday without having to go anywhere. Augmented-reality headsets could change your house and normal surroundings into something very different. Perhaps the kitchen will become a fish-filled coral lagoon, while the living room is a crystal cave!

IN THE POOL

10 YEARS

One of the best things to do on holiday is take a dip in the pool or swim in the warm sea. Many people take lessons in SCUBA diving while on holiday, learning how to breathe air from a tank. In future, artificial gills could make breathing underwater a lot easier. These would use thin membranes to separate out the oxygen gas mixed into water. They would use the same process that makes gas bubble out of fizzy drinks when you open the lid. We would then breathe the released oxygen through a mouthpiece similar to the one used by divers today. Just think, you could spend all day in the pool – sitting on the bottom.

GLOSSARY

3D Short for three-dimensional; when a flat picture on a screen (or even paper) is presented in such a way that it looks like it is a real object, with length, width but also depth.

app Short for application, an app is a small program that does one or perhaps a few simple jobs.

artificial Made by people; the opposite of natural.

audible Something that can be heard.

augmented reality When ordinary reality, such as the view around us or the pages of a book or magazine, is added to (or augmented) by content from a computer.

BASE jumper A daredevil parachutist who does not jump out of aircraft, but leaps from tall things, such as Buildings, Antennas, Spans (or bridges) and Earth features (like cliffs).

Darwin Charles Darwin was an English scientist who came up with the theory of evolution.

evolve To change by a process of evolution. Evolution acts on groups that are similar but slightly different. Some differences make certain members successful, while others do not, so the good differences become more common.

exoskeleton A skeleton that is on the outside of the body; human bones form an endoskeleton, on the inside of the body. A crab's tough shell is an exoskeleton, and a wearable robot is also a kind of exoskeleton.

fungus A lifeform similar to a plant, but which cannot make its own food; fungi include types of mould, yeast and mushrooms.

gecko A type of lizard; most geckos have flat pads on their toes, which allow them to climb by sticking to flat surfaces.

gills The feathery organs that many organisms, such as fish and octopuses, use to extract oxygen from water and put it into the blood.

hologram A 3D image.

inkjet A type of printer where the ink - or other liquid - is squirted through tiny holes to create patterns of minute dots.

LED A light-emitting diode; an electronic component that gives out a beam of light when electricity flows through it.

software The programs and applications that make a computer work; the hardware refers to the microchips, screens and keyboards etc.

supercomputer A powerful computer that is made up of several - or perhaps hundreds - of processors working together. A normal computer has between one and four processors.

technology Using scientific knowledge to make useful tools.

USEFUL WEBSITES:

Listen to some evolving music, and get involved yourself:
darwintunes.org/

An invisibility cloak is shown in this video, although it is quite hard to see:
www.youtube.com/
watch?v=PD83dqSfCOY

Discover a whole new way of writing stories using 'telescopic' text:
www.telescopictext.org/

INDEX